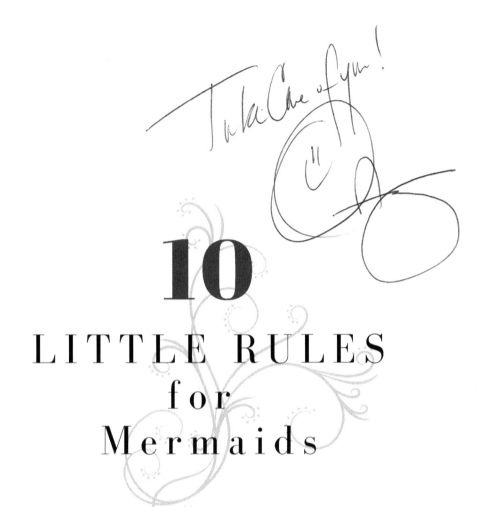

Take Care of you!

10
LITTLE RULES
for
Mermaids

by Amy Hege Atwell

ISBN-13: 978-0-9974799-6-6

For more information visit www.10littlerules.com

dedication

To my dear friend and mentor Stanley Spain.
For your wonderful humor and heart felt hugs
I will forever be grateful.
Namaste.

acknowledgements

I am so grateful for the variety of friends who have reached out almost daily through parts of all of this. And for those who took and continue to take my calls or messages at the most random times and have never once rushed me through the tears, and those who offered such simple words of wisdom and brilliance that got me back on track and able to move on with my day and in so many cases, laughing.

Many, many, thanks to the shoppers, artists, consigners, friends, fellow philosophers and followers of The Painted Mermaid without whom none of this would have happened as thoroughly or as completely.

To my "Immediate Mermaids," I absolutely cannot imagine life without you. As we move into our next chapters after the COVID-19 pandemic of 2020, please know that you have brought me much happiness and much peace, and for that I will be forever grateful.

And for the one who made me laugh in the beginning. I missed that SO terribly and am SO grateful that it's back. Thank you for being the start of what has indeed become, without a doubt, the most developmental chapter of my life. I'm sure you missed it, but this one was for you.

From the Painted Mermaid's blog, November 2, 2019

When I am my most tired and overwhelmed, reading will often
help settle my thoughts, and sometimes even put them into
words. As I am scrolling through hundreds of deep and
meaningful messages and quotes, one literally made me laugh
out loud, and something clicked. It's the laughter, Sunshine.
It's the laughter that you're missing.
It's the laughter that draws you in and holds you.
It's the laughter that hugs your heart.
It's the laughter that takes you places and keeps you there.
And it's the laughter that hurts the most when it's taken away.
It's not so much those who 'JUST' make you laugh at THEIR
jokes, but those who ALSO laugh at YOURS. This exchange,
it's the witty banter, it's the back and forth …
For me, laughter is the fastest way to feel and BE attractive …
It helps reset and regroup. It can soften pain.
Laughter helps heal. So just know it's OK, Sunshine.
It really is. Laughter is a GOOD thing and what it does for
EVERYONE around you is just as important
as what it does for you …
See you when you get here.

table of contents

foreword

What do you say when the right person at the right time crosses your path in exactly the right way? There are no words in that moment, only a deep recognition of the "rightness" of the idea.

So it was when Amy and I crossed paths and first talked about this book. From the start her energy was undeniable, her spirit was magical, her sass was off the charts ... I knew I had found "my mermaid."

As our collaboration took shape, so has a beautiful friendship, a partnership in the best sense, imbued with a deep respect for each other and what we can create together in this shared space.

It's been a journey for both of us to create something ... wild ... during these oh so wild days of 2020. Worldwide pandemic? Let's start a pandemic of another sort, and join the movement to empower all souls to live a life of depth, freedom and joy.

Carol Pearson
Founder, 10 Little Rules
www.10littlerules.com

I was just out taking pictures of the Moon and I had the thought that if you just glance at her, she's beautiful.

But if you look closer, you see all the scars she carries and damage she has survived.

For me, that makes her even more beautiful.

Just thinking.

~ Andy Birkey

introduction

As I was turning the corner, thinking I was close to wrapping up this book and sending it off to the editor, I sent a copy to a friend who offered the very simple observation: "Do you introduce yourself (and the store) somewhere at the beginning?"

Ah yes, that ...

My name is Amy Hege Atwell. I started in retail when I was 16; I got keys to my first building when I was 19. Shortly thereafter I started announcing that one day I wanted to "own my own store so that I can either make the millions I think I can or be humbled enough to go back to work for 'the man', whichever comes first." In 2010, after years of selling goodies picked from yard sales and thrift shops on the side or, better yet, gifted by friends, I finally had the opportunity to do just that. With the help of my new friend Marcie Newman Fiske, I opened The Painted Mermaid.

For two years Marcie did the day-to-day while I held onto my corporate "big box retail" position as a Human Resource executive for Target. It was such a wonderful, simple time. I will always remember the squeals from both of us the first day we did over $100 in sales, the rearranging together on my days off, and running up and down the island in the evenings looking for discarded treasures along the side of the road.

Then in 2011, when I was 42, my husband and I found out we were expecting. After having been told this wasn't possible, I was ecstatic.

Yet I knew without a doubt that staying in corporate retail would mean rarely seeing the child I had waited so long to bring into the world. So I made plans to come work at "The Mermaid" full time. When my baby was three weeks old, we did just that, together.

Because we were not yet at a point where sales could support multiple players, Marcie graciously went on to other things while my tiny baby and I worked open to close, seven days a week. Dave DeGroat, our resident woodcarver who had found us four days after opening ("I carve mermaids. Would you like to see some?"), was readily available to help with the munchkin if we got busy. Shoppers – many of whom were, by that point, family – came to visit and play, and "The Mermaid" took on a whole new layer.

We took consignments from local artists and welcomed second-hand treasures from those cleaning closets and attics. I continued to "pick" thrift shops when I could, and at some point started painting furniture with a new product called chalk paint. (Yes, the name The Painted Mermaid came long before the paint). We had a crib – then later a high chair – behind the counter, diapers stashed next to the bags, toys, bottles and books … I can't think of a better way to have escaped corporate America or to spend the first years of my baby's life. It was indeed the perfect way for me to be my version of "stay at home Mom."

Fast forward to 2017, the year my world shifted … just ever so slightly. In fact, almost imperceptibly, but just enough. New thought processes were introduced, awareness to shortcomings was heightened, the need for change was recognized, and a newfound confidence grew. The next two years became a whirlwind of realizing, and spinning into practice 32 years of experience, ideas and plans in the form of a second location for my lifelong dream The Painted Mermaid.

And then came 2018 and 2019, and with it Hurricanes Florence, Michael, and Dorian, followed closely by the temporary closing of the

Oak Island Bridge.

Once again things shifted – this times a bit more dramatically. The timing and combination of the storms and the bridge closure sent me down a financial path that was completely unexpected; a path that wound through terrible health issues resulting from an undiagnosed food allergy, and a tense marriage. My dream and my business were on shaky ground.

Then came the realization of amazing health through serious dietary changes, the development of a love of exercise, the gift of the practice of yoga, and the discovery of author Tosha Silver, all ultimately culminating in the sale of our home in the second half of 2019. Plans to build a new home hung in limbo, while a serious surgical injury and a separation from my husband of 23 years (after 27 years together) all happened during the Thanksgiving and Christmas holidays.

Throughout that period I began to feel the NEED to write, and began to put into words the thoughts that came to me, often in the middle of the night, in the form of blog posts on The Painted Mermaid page. The reaction was both rewarding and validating and without realizing it, my personal "policies" or "rules" began to amplify, take shape and solidify. Encouraged by dear friend and author Stanley Spain, I began to think my interest in writing might actually be realized.

At some point during all of this I noticed what appeared to be one business not only sharing my blog posts but commenting on them as well. Flattered – and curious – I clicked on the page, and then the website. After reading the intro – completely on impulse and totally out of character – I emailed the business, stating that it seemed as if we were of "like minds," that I'd had thoughts of a book for years, and that perhaps we should talk.

Within minutes publisher Carol Pearson, founder of 10 Little Rules, responded and shared that she'd had the working title 10 Little Rules for Mermaids on her "bucket list" of concepts for some time now and that she had been thinking she "may have found her mermaid."

I don't know which one of us confessed having chills first, but I do remember having tears in my eyes. All very dramatic I know, but I learned a long time ago never to argue with fate – we agreed we should meet and discuss a book.

At that exact moment I was just coming through what should have been a very simple medical procedure gone frighteningly awry, ending in a full blown surgery with an anticipated eight-week recovery. My husband and I had just separated and, although all of this brought so many closer in around me and still others unexpectedly to the forefront, I was completely unprepared for how the separation in particular was changing the dynamic of virtually every relationship. People were shocked. Some friends began to step back or pull away. I was mourning that loss in addition to the obvious.

People began to share things about their own relationships, asking questions, pointing out that "we weren't the only ones". I began to joke that I had become the "self-proclaimed patron saint of all women slighted." My writing became "heavier" and it was clear that what I had thought would be a simple "gathering and enhancing" of my blog posts to form the book would have to be more than that.

I began nattering to Carol about "talking to Neptune instead of Sunshine" (referring to how my blog posts had taken form); I knew I wanted to help men understand us as women. (Really, Amy??) I continued to feel as if, to borrow an expression from my friend and fellow artist Bess, it all "needed to come out." I just couldn't tap into how or with what words. Finally, at some point, I grasped that none of it was mine to decide. The book needed to come just like my posts had – in its own sweet time, at its own sweet pace and just exactly as it damn well pleased.

Finally, I thought to ask Carol what her inspiration for the working title had been. She spoke of being "drawn to mermaids before mermaids became so mainstream" and "wondering what it is about mermaids that draws us to the idea." Was it about the water? Or was it more about their freedom? Maybe a combination of both?

As she talked out loud, so many of our thoughts overlapped that I struggle to remember which were her words and which my own. I had always wanted to be a mermaid when I grew up; for me that was always without a doubt about the water and the feeling that came with diving in, floating on, simply being in absolutely any kind of water. Yet the word freedom stuck with me during the conversation, planted itself and grew in my head. I've since realized that, for the first time in 27 years (literally more than half my life) I have the complete freedom to work on me – without feeling compelled to do the same with or for anyone else.

Although quite overwhelming at times, I now know that I will do everything in my power to never sacrifice that freedom again. And the chances of that actually happening have increased a thousand times over since I now realize no one ever ASKED me to give up my freedom in the first place – I just did that on my own. I did it for jobs, I did it for my marriage, and I did it to myself. I did that very wrong thing for all the right reasons ... and now I find myself wondering ... how do you STAY free? How does one regain said freedom if it's been lost in a relationship? How do you rediscover it after you've left a relationship? And how in the world do you retain it if you're entering a new one?

Questions turn into answers in their own sweet time, and I woke up completely refreshed at 2 a.m. this morning, feeling like today is the day to start pulling it all together – the book that is; I've been working on the life part MUCH longer than that! It has been unbelievably cleansing to put my thoughts into writing, to get them out of my head and to share them with the universe, both publicly and privately.

As you read my words, my 10 Little Rules for Mermaids if you will, I hope they will help you do the same for yourself. Write your thoughts down, in single words or broken sentences even. Dog ear this book; write in this book; highlight, color, circle and draw in this book, absolutely all over, under and through this book. Do what works for you. Make this book YOURS. After all, that is EXACTLY what freedom is all about.

Nice to meet you Mermaid, and thank you for being here.

RULE #1
back your own trailer

Everything about this new situation has made me that much more inclined to ask others their thoughts about their everyday lives and how they choose to live them. At some point, while chatting with an old friend, he commented that he thought he'd "feel grown by now." I truly don't remember how that came up, or where the conversation went from there, but the comment struck me then, and has stuck with me since. Not only because my impression of this person is that he has things pretty darn together in the world of 'being grown,' but because I can relate on so many levels.

As I've turned it over and over in my head, I've realized that I don't exactly NOT feel grown, but a little behind maybe? … or naïve for my age? … or not consistently pulled together? It's hard to put into words, but as I move through being newly single at 50 (or as my Daddy keeps pointing out, "almost 51, Punkin") I realize now more than ever how much I've looked to my husband in particular over our years together to somehow just know how to handle certain things – and how often I've just accepted so many decisions without challenge. How I somehow felt quite subconsciously that conceding to one's husband was how you did 'being grown.' Now, please don't get me wrong – I am EXTREMELY independent in SO many ways.

RULE #1
back your own trailer

I've run high dollar retail buildings from an early age, opened and run The Painted Mermaid in tandem with holding down a corporate level position and learned MANY things while moving and expanding that business. And I like to think I'm a pretty reasonable Mommy. And no, I've certainly not done any of this alone – I've had plenty of support from many wonderful people, including at times my husband, but for all intents and purposes he was rarely involved.

He was never one to accept a 'Honey do' list, let alone complete it, but when I needed a short cut, or didn't know where to start with something foreign like purchasing a new computer, I'd take his suggestions and rarely research it on my own. Yes, I recognized that I could have or maybe even should have done more on my own behalf, but if it ended up being wrong, it somehow felt 'less my fault' and I just didn't have time to dig around on my own. I rarely asked for help, but as lead times lengthened on his responses, I would say "teach me; that way I won't have to ask." With too much on both our plates, communication during the few times we tried this approach was tense at best, and I stopped asking.

I'd done extensive research in my last 'real world' position as a Human Resource Executive and began to recognize for the first time I could apply that skill for myself. Google is indeed a fabulous thing – add to that Pinterest and then (cue angels singing) YouTube and the world opens like nobody's business. I made it through small things like using Wi-Fi through the computer at the store to add a speaker for music, and when I decided I needed a tool, I researched and purchased it on my own. I was invited to 'join the maker community' and as a result, found many specialized Facebook pages that pertained to several needs at various times. Life became easier and I became

RULE #1
back your own trailer

more confident. Maybe even a little more "grown."

And then there was "The Trailer" … the beast that was becoming more and more huge from a "critical to the business" standpoint. I could pull it comfortably and was beginning to feel more confident about actually hooking it up, but backing it continued to elude me. I could sort of back it in a real pinch, but there tended to always be a capable fellow in the places I frequented willing to hop in and 'speed things along' and I found myself often "relying on the kindness of strangers."

The turning point came after pulling into a parking lot with a girlfriend riding shotgun and not realizing the far end of the lot had been blocked off. For whatever reason my brain would NOT click with the maneuvers needed to get us out. At some point I even stopped, pulled out my phone and searched YouTube videos, all to no avail. Finally, we called her husband – who was able to offer something that registered just enough for me to regroup and back us out.

We had him on speaker, and I remember hearing him ask, while he had her on the phone, how to wash their child's hair (the child was 4 or 5 at the time) and my saying after they hung up that if he made fun of us, tell him that in all fairness to me I at least know how to wash my child's hair. Yet later I thought about the fact that EVERYONE must learn something new sometimes, EVEN MEN. And although waiting four years to jump in on something as seemingly basic as washing your child's hair might seem way overdue, he and I had essentially been doing the same thing, just sailing along letting someone else handle an important function of daily life, taking for granted that help would always be there. So just like I had just gotten in there and figured out how to wash my own little one's hair without having him slip out of my hands or getting soap in his eyes, I was just going to have to make it

RULE #1
back your own trailer

my mission to practice backing that trailer until I could do it as well as ANYONE else. I'm sure I wasted AT LEAST an hour and certainly no less than a quarter of a tank of gas doing it, but we did eventually escape that parking lot, and I did so feeling just a little more "grown."

After that I began sucking up my pride and telling those helpful men "thank you anyway, but I was learning" when they offered to back it for me. I even learned to deal with it when some of them wanted to stand there and watch (fighting the urge on more than one occasion to throw out that line from Pretty Woman about charging extra to watch) and it was always WAY worse when the person watching was my husband.

But by golly, eventually it got to the point that not only was I able to get it done in under half an hour and an eighth of a tank, but there was even the occasional compliment offered by a much older gentlemen (typically followed up with the added bonus of 'young lady') or even a much younger man who would simply offer a 'wow' when someone his mother's age got out of the truck – both extremely rewarding.

And then there was the very simple compliment of "nice work," offered almost in passing by a new friend after directing me into an extremely tricky situation in a lot full of trucks and trailers, with the clock ticking.

The comments that register the most these days though are those from other women. It's not only with the trailer; sometimes it's with things like tools or repair. It's the women who say things like "wow, I never even thought about doing that myself," or "I'd go ahead and buy it but I doubt I could get my husband to hang it" that get my attention.

This works in the other direction as well — my Daddy saying "I never really learned how to cook, Punkin', Jane always did that," and other men saying, "I don't know, I let my wife handle all that" when it comes to something as simple as whether or not they like a

RULE #1
back your own trailer

certain piece of furniture. (For the record, I'd like to point out that I am sure these women know how to do PLENTY of other things, just as my Daddy does indeed know how to cook, and these other fellows probably do have their own opinions even if they've forgotten, however briefly, what those opinions may be.)

Here's my point. If you want something, don't wait for someone else to do it or get it for you. Don't just speak to finding some class or assume you can't afford it, if it even exists. Google it, ask around, phone a friend. You'd be amazed what you may stumble upon just by asking – who has the same interests, who is willing to teach, and how much you may already know without even realizing it. That, my friend, is now my definition of what it means to be 'grown.' It's not a matter of having it all together all the time, or feeling confident in EVERY situation, but that ability to do what it takes to take care of YOU, to actually take the steps, no matter how small, to actually put yourself closer to whatever it is that is important to you … for WHATEVER reason.

It's learning the difference between helping and crippling yourself, your partner or your child. It's knowing when to step in without having to be told when another needs attention or care.

It's the asking when you're unsure and being careful to leave no relevant topics un-tapped. It's the apologizing when you've mis-stepped and it's the knowing when and how to move on for your own development. And it's the knowing that in many cases someone's reaction to you really does have precious little to do with you and instead more to do with their own confidence or lack thereof. Just know that with a bit of nerve and a lot of practice, you too can learn to back your own trailer, Mermaid, and anything else you darn well please! So carpe diem and I'll see you when you get here.

Amy Hege Atwell

your turn ...

back your own trailer

What skill do you lack that keeps you from doing something that is important to you, or keeps you reliant on someone else?

What REALLY keeps you from learning that skill? (Is it a lack of confidence? lack of support from a significant other?)

What steps can you take to change this?

Use the journal space on the next few pages to write down your thoughts and ideas.

1

back your own trailer

date _____

1

back your own trailer

date _____

Amy Hege Atwell

RULE #2
find your community

The word community has literally been used with me three times in the last two days. The first came from a wise friend as we were discussing the way my little one had tried to communicate the difference between being with me at our house and at Daddy's. He mentioned Daddy's house as having "more than one grownup" (my husband shares a house with his mother and a friend).

The more he and I talked, the more I realized if one person couldn't give him full attention while cooking dinner or whatever, another did. My friend had assessed that as "ok, so he's looking for community, and that may not just be in the form of adults; he may need more play dates or whatever."

The second reference came from another friend (in fact the mommy of the play date I'd arranged as a result of conversation number one) discussing ways she enjoys her home being open and therefore the hub, if you will, of her community – her words were loosely about "loving community and being surrounded by people" and not that it gave her value, but how it gave her value. At this point the universe had my attention, and when my dear friend and fellow business owner of Seaglass Salvage Market, Kelli Benton, (aka 'Kelli Seaglass') applied it in terms of what she and I were trying to build both

RULE #2
find your community

separately and together, the thoughts fell into place.

My husband and I spent our early years surrounded by community – we lived with his parents and had a large group of friends with whom we were always socializing. I was and continue to be a talker, a sharer of ideas, a collaborator. He, on the other hand, has always tended to lean toward 'let's just sit and watch TV.' So, in the beginning there was always someone to not only listen when I needed to talk, but someone to talk back and with. Now, I don't want to take anything away from what was overall a good marriage. We had a lot of good years together, have a beautiful son and are at this writing functioning together better in many ways as co-parents than we ever did as a married couple, but 'talking' was never really our thing.

Yet it wasn't until after separating I began to realize that I had never really given myself a chance to be on my own, which is of course different from spending time alone, although to a degree the two go hand in hand. When we moved and this community dwindled away, our foundation as a couple changed, and my identity as an individual became that much more about my career. When we became pregnant at 42 and I left the 'real' work world to become a full time mermaid, the adjustments were profound. At some point I finally realized there were chunks of me that had not only disappeared, but that I truly missed.

Post from the Painted Mermaid, December 11, 2019
"Keep taking time for yourself til you're you again" -- Lalah Delia
Ahhh this ... taking time ... "When I get to a good stopping point" ...
"When I get this last thing (or 12) off my list" ... "When my husband /son,
daughter / wife gets through their thing" ... THEN I'll take some time.
But somewhere in and amongst all that, you start to lose you. Not

RULE #2
find your community

necessarily in a core values kind of way, but in an "I'm not even sure what I'd do with myself if I had the time" kind of way. And that is so not good, Sunshine. Not good for you, and not good for those around you.
One of my favorite analogies is of the directions given before a flight where in case of an emergency you're instructed to "put on your OWN air mask, BEFORE assisting others." Doing so allows you to help others more effectively. In other words – and I love this line from an article in The Associated Press – "You'll be of no use if you pass out from oxygen deprivation."
I for one believe it's the same for "pleasure in life deprivation."
Of course there has to be a balance, and an exception to every rule, but at the end of the day I think what it boils down to is that most of us are good at recognizing we HAVE those needs; it's the drilling down to the roots and the specifics and ACTING on them where we drop the ball.
So take a minute today to just do something no one asked you to do, something not on your mandated and often self-imposed to-do list. Take a walk just to see close up what's happening on the block outside your office. Sit and LISTEN to the WHOLE song, or better yet, SING it. Lock your phone in your car for 30 minutes while you eat, taste and actually ENJOY a GOOD meal. It doesn't have to be much, but every little bit counts. So little snippets Sunshine, keep taking little snippets until you're you again, and you just may be surprised at how much easier it ALL becomes.

I call myself an extroverted introvert and I do love my time solo, but thanks to my FABULOUS community and modern technology, there is always someone with whom to check in or make light conversation via text or message, and I would not change that for the world – these people know, love and accept me and my ridiculous self just the way I am, and I know, love and accept them all right back!! But something I

RULE #2
find your community

have now added to my 'make time for' routine is the setting aside of
the phone, maybe even leaving it in the other room, and freeing myself
completely of outside influences. I allow myself time for yoga and
music and reading and researching things in which I am interested. I
unplug while spending time with my little one – and explain to him
when I am not, why that is. And I am realizing more and more that if I
am going to be a fabulous mother to my child and a wonderful co-
parent with his father, a great friend to my community and a strong
and successful business owner in EVERY way then taking care of ME
is the single most important thing I can do – and finding my tribe, my
support team, MY communities (not JUST my husband's or my son's)
has and will continue to be a HUGE part of that.

So don't put all your eggs in one basket Mermaid. Know that the
person you married may or may not be able to fulfill EVERY need
ALL the time – decide, then communicate how much of that is or isn't
OK for you. Give yourself the freedom to figure out who, without
breaking any vows, either literally or figuratively, may be a stronger
partner for some of your needs. Don't let your partner completely off
the hook, and don't inadvertently leave them completely out of your
loop. By the same token, pay attention. If you realize you are the one
who has been left, find out WHY and DO something about it. As you
evolve and grow, know that others around you may or may not choose
to grow in the same direction, and that is OK. Surround yourself with
great community, without sacrificing your ability to be alone and on
your own, all the while remembering it may take a village to raise a
child, and a community to nurture an adult, but only YOU can find
YOU.

See you when you get here.

your turn ...

find
your
community

What gaps do you need to fill in your community of friends?

Where can you go to start to fill those gaps? (classes? lectures? sports groups? play dates with children/grandchildren?)

Have you expressed this need (if applicable) to your spouse or partner?

date _____

find your community

date _____

date _____

find your community

date _____

Amy Hege Atwell

RULE #3
speak slowly and clearly

I don't know who actually told me the joke first, but I give my Daddy the credit. It's the one where two guys are driving down the road. The first guy says, "I'm telling you we are in Georgia."

The second argues back, "No, we're in South Carolina."

"Georgia."

"South Carolina."

The fellow driving says, "I'll tell you what, next chance we get, we'll pull over and ask somebody."

A couple of miles down the road they spot an exit and pull in somewhere to ask where they are. They go up to the counter and say to the woman working, "We hope you can help us settle something." Enunciating clearly he says, "Very slowly and clearly, please tell us where – we – are."

And very slowly and very clearly, the woman responds.

"Bur – ger – King."

At this point I remember my Daddy cracking himself up. It will always be one of my favorite jokes to trot out to make a point.

People don't get it, Mermaid. They don't get the hints. They don't understand that the scooping up of your jacket and purse before moving to a table across the room was because they were talking too

RULE #3
speak slowly and clearly

loudly – no one gets that, and sadly they often don't care. Men in particular often state they aren't mind readers, and no, no they aren't. No one is.

The older I get the more likely I am to just spit whatever it is out – and oh my goodness what a difference. Now I DO NOT mean that it's OK to be mean, or rude, or the wrong kind of blunt, but the days of dropping hints or hoping someone will notice, let alone read the deep meaning behind a look on my face, are rapidly becoming a thing of the past. By the same token, I ask for and expect the same from those around me. And if they actually have the nerve to do it, I welcome it and do my damnedest to make sure I don't punish them even a little bit for doing what I asked – even if it happens to be delivered awkwardly, or in altogether the wrong way.

I'd say that COMMUNICATION is the single most critical aspect of ANY relationship, Mermaid, and often we just don't give it. We spend so much time complaining to each other instead of just saying what we need – or for the love of Pete, even SHOWING if it comes right down to it – that we often don't get the point across to the person who needs it the most. Or we don't make it clear just what level of CRITICAL the situation may be or how devastating its impact. So Speak Slowly and Clearly, Mermaid. And when whatever it is happens again, or the person on the receiving end doesn't compute, repeat and REPHRASE. Make your limits ABUNDANTLY clear and let them know on which strike they are now.

I received this snarky retort one time from a friend who had been taking advantage of our friendship: "what, am I on PROBATION now?" To which I replied, "No, you've BEEN on probation; the next

RULE #3
speak slowly and clearly

time you're OUT."

We are still friends to this day and our friendship is stronger as a result. Recognize that you are probably not going to change someone's core values, nor should you expect to, so figure out for yourself what it is that you may be willing to compromise WITHOUT RESENTMENT. And never – and I do mean never – make a promise you aren't fully prepared to keep – with adults, with children, or even yourself – because when you've spoken slowly and you've spoken clearly one too many times, it's time to make good on said promise. If you don't, just know you run the risk of losing all credibility. If it's important enough to make the threat, Mermaid, it's important to make good.

See you when you get here.

Amy Hege Atwell

your turn ...

speak slowly and clearly

What is your greatest strength as a communicator?

What are your opportunities for growth in this area?

Do you seem to have repeated issues in certain areas, at home, school, work or with friends?

If you could magically change one thing about your tendencies/results, what would that be?

If you've examined all of these pieces of yourself and there is no other person/topic/trigger that is common to them, is the 'problem' really you?

3

speak slowly & clearly

3

speak slowly & clearly

date _____

date _____

Amy Hege Atwell

RULE #4
cure what ails you

It's interesting what puts you down what path. As I sit not only reviewing my most recent years in detail, but putting chunks of it down on paper, I realize that strangely enough getting healthy was the beginning of the end in more ways than one – the end of what had become not only stagnant, but detrimental, and the beginning of what has now grown into one of the most empowering and rewarding parts of my (insert REALLY big word here) life – existence – core.

I'd have to really drill down the calendar to find a date, but sometime in early 2016 I began having terrible pain and constipation (nothing awkward about sharing that with the world!) that eventually turned into horrible room spinning dizziness, violent throwing up and finally into hours or even days where I literally could not stand. I could barely speak to communicate to any observer what was happening. My husband was great through parts of this and each time I stammered out "call 911" he did.

Now, just to paint the picture, I have always been a "no, no, it's just a flesh wound, we don't need to see a doctor, I'll just bite the knife while you tie the tourniquet and we'll finish digging the ditch" kind of gal, but this was AWFUL. And no one could tell me what was wrong. My husband would correct me in the emergency room when asked things like "how long has it been since you've been to the bathroom." I would say "maybe a week?" He would tell them more

RULE #4
cure what ails you

like three, and their response would be something like, "well your body will have to go at some point so just do clear liquids for a couple of days to give it a rest, take a softener if you feel like you need to and you should be fine." (insert horrified emoji here!?!)

So on I went, searching for answers but finding none. I eventually found a fabulous PA who was truly horrified at what he was hearing and sent me to a gastroenterologist who told me, "Well it's great that you're drinking more water, but that's not going to solve your problems, and you're too young for Metamucil, so here try this $400-a-month prescription and take it indefinitely."

When I asked about my body becoming reliant on it, he positively told me not to worry. But I felt like he thought I was asking about becoming a crack fiend when I just wanted to make sure that if we eventually found other ways to correct the problem, having gone "this route" wouldn't create more damage.

Clearly, he thought we were done, but being someone who has never been a fan of automatically resorting to medication, I began to research on my own behalf. I finally thought to partner with my amazing friend and Certified Traditional Herbalist Lyndsey Hughes, who listened to my symptoms then offered, "That sounds like either dairy or wheat. Eliminate one for a while and see what that does for you."

Desperate to fix it quickly I tried to fast forward by eliminating both at once but realized my mistake and stepped back to just the dairy. At first eliminating just the obvious – no cheese, no butter, no milk – I couldn't BELIEVE the difference. Within days I stopped feeling nauseous, trips to the bathroom improved and I started dropping the

RULE #4
cure what ails you

mysterious water weight I had been carrying like crazy. Encouraged, I searched all words dairy and began reading labels.

I ate nothing that contained casein, whey, lactose, lactate (why exactly is there dairy in deli meat and hotdogs??) and holy cow I began to feel like a whole new person. I also noticed that my anxiety, my moodiness and quick temper – all things I had chalked up to stress or being perimenopausal – were gone. Eventually I grasped that eating foods without labels, like fresh fruits and vegetables (because let's be honest, no one NEEDS a hotdog), made things SIMPLE and quite frankly less terrifying. (If that's not milk in that creamy cookie center my friend, what is it???) My practical mind wondered if it was a coincidence, but I just couldn't work up the nerve to put it to the test. Then dinner at my mother-in-law's answered the question.

She is a true southern cook and I had been honored at just how far out of her norm she had gone to accommodate my new needs. But a miscommunication about ingredients resulted in stomach-churning, room spinning dizziness. We didn't discuss what was in the sauce she'd made for the sweet potatoes and I somehow decided on my own that it had been made with water and sugar, instead of cream. I was grateful for the answer and relieved that it wasn't worse, but quite frankly saddened and depressed with the realization that for sure now there would be no more ice cream, no more ranch dressing, no more pizza. I busied myself with altering recipes and researching lifestyles such as vegetarianism.

And then I stumbled on to the Paleo Lifestyle. All the information about the danger from grains and processed foods made SO much sense to me. Having something on which to focus was a huge relief, as

RULE #4
cure what ails you

were the improvements in my EVERYTHING! My brain fog went away, my memory improved, my joint pain disappeared (I had at one point been diagnosed with fibromyalgia – I no longer consider that the case). I could go on and on.

I am quick to tell folks that were it not for the fact that dairy will LITERALLY put me down almost immediately – for as long as 24 hours – and that I truly should not be alone until it clears my system because I cannot stand or help myself with ANYTHING – I don't know if I would have been as quick to turn things around. But I like to think at some point things would have eventually clicked.

Embracing the whole concept and learning the WHYS behind it all has been incredibly eye opening. Going at my health from the aspect of HEALTH, and not how I looked in a bathing suit, changed EVERYTHING, not just for me but with how I did things with my little guy. Like most mommies I had always been big on minimizing sugar, but I lunged into that much further as well as NO ARTIFICIAL sweeteners (I use NATURAL LOCAL honey when baking and making smoothies) and was thrilled when, after removing dairy from his diet, the mother of one of his little buddies was able to greatly improve some of her little guy's behaviors in school and reduce his ADHD medications (all with guidance from medical professionals, of course).

Although in so many ways I would prefer to, I haven't COMPLETELY removed things like cheese sticks and pizza from my guy's diet. And we do indulge in fast food on occasion (Bo Rounds are indeed my kryptonite), but I know for me having something be taboo has always made it that much more tempting, and why do that to a child? He and I talk about what is good for us and what should be

RULE #4
cure what ails you

done in moderation and these things are on that list. Keeping my system super clean on a regular basis has made it easy to know how much worse I feel after said treat, and that most certainly helps keep temptation at bay.

So let me put this out there to you – making YOU your mission should absolutely include your health. I frequently hear how expensive it is to eat healthy, but take a minute and write down the money you're spending on fast food or a glass of wine every night, that bladder buster diet soda or a pint of non-dairy ice cream after the little ones go to bed (not that I've ever done that myself – clears throat). That's a lot of money that could just as easily be spent on fresh fruits and vegetables. I believe you will be completely shocked at just how amazing these clean foods taste after you purge your system of what ails you. I actually CRAVE fruit these days. Prepackaged non-homemade cookies truly don't even SOUND good.

Being in control of what you eat has a strange way of putting you in control of many other aspects of your life. And all those things that used to worry me – being a burden on whoever was cooking dinner, not wanting to be left out, feeling awkward with wait staff – has all gone away and no longer worries me. Because as the world catches up to the idea that we all don't or can't eat the same, restaurants are MUCH better equipped to accommodate. AND IT'S MY HEALTH!!

So if you have concerns, Mermaid, take control. Paleo may not be your answer, but sometimes just having a place to start can put you down an interesting path to what is. As you embark on your journey, never forget, you can lead by example, but you can't force change in others (your children being an exception, and sneaking in the good

RULE #4
cure what ails you

food balances the body and pretty quickly reduces their taste for sugars and the like – but that's a whole different book).

If those around you don't support you or follow your lead for whatever reason, the answers will come. You'll just know. And when you do, you will be in a much better place to feel stronger and more comfortable doing and being with what, and who, is right for you.

So here's to good health, Mermaid! See you when you get here.

your turn ...

cure
what
ails
you

What do you want/need to change about your health?

What has worked in your past?

What hasn't? Why?

What change in circumstances or mindset might make a difference?

What new simple steps might you take? (read new materials? focus on long term change vs. quick fix?)

4

cure what ails you

date _____

4

cure what ails you

date _____

Amy Hege Atwell

RULE #5
know you're not the only one

As women, I think we tend to have two modes of sharing. There's the "I am way too embarrassed to share this with ANYBODY except MAYBE my mother," and then there's the "I can't help it but I need to talk with ANYONE who will listen, up to and including the cashier at Walmart."

Even as I grow older (and wiser ?), I waffle back and forth and tend to be extremely relieved and horribly embarrassed all at the same time when I develop a case of diarrhea of the mouth. But the last going on – oh my gosh, 2 years?? – have been wall-to-wall, action-packed with back to back 'are you kidding me??' events ... for myself, and for those closest around me. As a result, I've all but embraced the nattering. I like to think I'm not the only one it has helped. Others have opened up and offered great stories of their own experiences, and in many cases asked key questions that have made me really think through mine. Yet I am proud to report that for whatever reason – probably being in share mode only regarding certain topics – all CRITICAL decisions have been made by me with very little to no outside influence of opinions. After all, you really do have to be VERY cautious about who you invite inside your head!

My most important take away from all of this has been that you are

RULE #5
know you're not the only one

rarely – IF EVER – the only one who is or has gone through whatever it is. I often use the analogy that we as women don't always tell each other, for example, that nursing a baby, no matter how amazingly rewarding, isn't always easy. And if for whatever reason you can't have a child – or God help us, don't want to – we don't share how hard BOTH are. (I spent 18 years of our marriage fielding the "when are you going to" questions and waffling dramatically between acceptance and despair until God gifted me with the birth of my child at 42). The other thing we rarely offer each other unsolicited is the fact that during the course of a marriage, frequency sometimes changes. (In our case, I could pinpoint almost exactly the date of my son's conception.) Sometimes I was able to set the lack of physical connection aside, but more often than not, it was hurtful.

We don't talk about how it's not really the swinging from the trees of it all that we miss (or I have now been told by MULTIPLE sources, NEVER HAD), but the CONNECTION, a word offered by a friend trying to help me put my thoughts into words. Another offered the word COMPANIONSHIP when drilling down to what would take priority if one was forced to choose. Yet a third challenged "what's wrong with wanting the total package?"

As I carefully shared what changes were happening for us, many friends offered their own experiences, and through conversation I like to think we were able to validate each other's thoughts, worries, and concerns – by knowing we weren't alone in the experience, it became more clear that it truly wasn't ALL about US or how our partners felt about US, but that more often than not, it was about what was happening with THEM. Each of us then had to take what we wanted

RULE #5
know you're not the only one

from each conversation and leave the rest – go home and do with it what felt right to each of us in our own unique circumstances, knowing, I hope, that more open conversation either with each other or our partners, may be the one thing that increases our chances of a "permanent fix," (realizing at the same time that sometimes the "permanent fix" is compromise, agreeing to disagree, or truly being OK with just being OK).

It's amazing just how often in my current circumstances my thoughts turn to what might have made a difference for this go round and what will be OK if and when I choose to embark on a next; how often I think about how to convey any of this to my male child as he grows into a young man; and what if anything I might feel important to offer his future partner or bride (and knowing that what I say to either of them could quite possibly be taken far too literally or as "crossing a line"). That's a lot of thoughts surrounding what is still a long way off, but we all want the very best for our children, and I do so hope that whoever joins him in life will feel comfortable coming to me with whatever they may need.

I feel quite strongly that it is our responsibility as women to offer up our experiences as openly as possible where and when we are able ... to male and female, experienced and inexperienced, young and old, indeed anyone in need of support (changing the names to protect the innocent where applicable). We must always remember that, more often than not, ALL of us have experienced SOMETHING similar. We have been made nervous or worse at the hands of a friend, date or employer. We have more than likely been hurt deeply by even a well-meaning boyfriend, spouse or parent. We have all done things we regret and would change the way we handled things if given the

RULE #5
know you're not the only one

chance. We evolve not only from those experiences, but from how we help others with what we've learned.

So know that you are not the only one, Mermaid, in WHATEVER the situation. Do your very best with the experience and information with which you have to work, in the moment in which you are. Take partners, ask questions, seek to understand. And when you come out stronger on the other side for having lived through it, forgive yourself for not knowing then what you know now. Pay your experience forward; doing so gives you power over whatever it was that hurt you, and closure. And that my friend is one of the very most important things YOU can do for YOU.

Namaste, Mermaid. See you when you get here.

your turn ...

know you're not the only one

What makes you feel alone?

To whom have you reached out about this?

How did that communication make you feel?

Did it give you a new direction?

What other resources might you explore? (Pinterest, Google search, library, support groups, church service, meditation?)

date _____

5

know you're not the only one

date _____

5

know you're not the only one

date _____

know you're not the only one

Amy Hege Atwell

RULE #6
find your zen

Early, early on in and amongst all of my recent challenges, I started losing my balance. I really didn't think much about it, just chalked it up to being clumsy and went about my business. But it was starting to happen a lot. Before the separation I had developed a routine of going into my studio or store in the middle of the night – the only time I could work uninterrupted without sacrificing time with my squirt. I would either go in after he fell asleep and work until I was about to fall over, or get up crazy early, work until it was time to get him up, then scoot home to get him ready and off to school. (Just so you can read the rest without being horrified and or distracted, yes, his Daddy was home.) There were a couple of times I fell – usually under a piece of furniture I was lifting on to my table or something equally DUMB to be doing alone in the middle of the night.

A work-out studio had moved in behind us (ironically into what had once been my studio) and I sought out the owner as a possible resource as to what might be happening. I decided to try a class or two myself, and as a way to support to another local business, I bought A LOT of gift certificates for work-out classes to give as prizes during our Black Friday event. Well, I'm pretty sure that it was a God thing that anyone who won the prize, didn't want it. Rather than

RULE #6
find your zen

keeping the prize or gifting to a friend, EVERY one of them opted to leave it with us. That, my friends, is the ONLY way I would have dared spend the money at all, let alone on myself. Instead the Universe decided for me, and off I went to balance classes. Now $8 a class felt like so much to spend back then, but every time I crumble and spend $8.73 or whatever it always is at the Wendy's drive through, I realize just how out of whack my train of thought had been my entire life.

Anyway ... I wasn't the only one in class who couldn't stand on one leg without all but toppling over. The whole experience was QUITE eye opening, and just like the whole thing with the dairy, it was absolutely unreal how quickly I began regaining my balance and developing strength. Several weeks into the class (that at my request had been planned around my schedule and level of ability) the instructor dared to change the time and increase the intensity level without consulting with me. I walked into the same time slot a couple of minutes late and straight into a "boot camp" class. Hesitantly I joined in – fit to be tied. I somehow survived until the end (truly it wasn't THAT much different; it was just the being caught off guard and "feeling trapped" or "too embarrassed to leave," – two triggers that I may NEVER overcome – threw me off COMPLETELY).

I made it back to my car and back to the house before dissolving into the most ridiculous level of teenaged girl behavior ever. I was so hurt and embarrassed. I actually felt so betrayed that she hadn't at least let me know ahead of time about the changes, that I SOBBED for a while before pulling my $h!t together and giving her a call. Or at least I thought I had. Now I'm sure there's something all very Freudian about that moment in time, but Freud was the furthest thing from my

RULE #6
find your zen

mind, and I was horrified when I started to cry ON THE PHONE. She
was, of course, horrified herself and apologized for having hurt my
feelings – that was certainly not the intention.

I nattered on about how for the first time in my life having a routine
together made me realize how much I needed this. Anyone listening
would have thought for sure she'd dumped me after having slept
together on prom night. Amazingly enough, we both got through the
conversation. Not only did she not file a restraining order, she
welcomed me back to class. Perhaps the true miracle here was that I
WENT. And when she "dared" to leave town on some personal
business for a couple of weeks, I made it through without crying! Like
a big girl, I began to connect the dots on not putting all my eggs in the
same work-out basket either.

The day after finding out about her upcoming trip, I was driving
down Oak Island Drive and the kiosk outside of the recreation center
was flashing YOGA FOR BALANCE as an upcoming class – at a time
I could make. That, ladies and gentlemen, was my next (quoting future
kick boxing instructor Shannon Gordon) "Jesus Slap" in just exactly
the right direction. There I met instructor Emily Silverman who was
just exactly the right addition to the mix and added yoga to my routine
– or, every bit of drama intended here – to my LIFE. I have come to
rely on yoga in so many ways and appreciate what it does for me
enough that I eventually figured out a way to practice at home alone
when needed. At some point I worked up the nerve to go to another
studio where everyone was as willing to teach as Emily (thank you,
Mert and Shannon of Rebel Soul). Then kickboxing sounded like fun,
so I mixed that in too (enter Candice Murphy and Shannon Gordon).

RULE #6
find your zen

So here's the thing, Mermaid. Being forced into doing these things has made me realize just how critical it is to take care of yourself in EVERY way. It's not selfish; it just makes sense. And if you're disciplined enough to do whatever it is on your own, please do! I have now added YouTube to my list of resources, and pulled out some of those old DVDs I'd bought literally a decade ago. But if you want or need outside help, and even coughing up $8 to get started feels tricky, consider this. Search the sofa, the floorboard, and the bottom of your purse. Put it on the list for when folks ask, "What do you want for your birthday?" Give up one fast food meal or bottle of wine and just give something – anything – a shot. Be realistic about where you are physically and be willing to start small and stick with it. And you know what? If you can make yourself do it, try it all by yourself. The buddy system never really worked for me. It was fun, but I tended to overdue with "reward" lunches, and in hindsight altogether missing the point. Doing all of this solo? Wow – talk about 'feeling grown!'

Make it about getting and staying healthy and the rest will come. And if a string bikini comes with it, great! More power to you, sister! But getting yourself to the point where you are comfortable in your own skin enough to take your new found strength and balance out to the beach, the swimming pool or even the dance floor is exactly what this should be about; the rest will come.

So invest in you and get out there and PLAY, Mermaid! Be just as active as you can possibly be in EVERY aspect of your life for just as long as you possibly can … and I'll see you when you get here.

your turn ...

find your zen

What brings you peace, calms you or keeps you from feeling anxious? What grounds you? (prayer? meditation? a hot bath? a call to a dear friend?)
What factors keep you from offering yourself this critical piece of self care?
What sources are available to you? (reading on the topic? yoga classes? walking or hiking for pleasure?)

6

find your zen

date _____

date _____

6

find your zen

date _____

Amy Hege Atwell

RULE #7
learn to laugh at yourself

They say what doesn't kill you makes you stronger, and in my case it made it a lot easier to finally grasp what really matters, and to let go of what does not. At this point EVERYTHING about daily life is MUCH easier. Less tense. Life is feeling lighter and I am once again actively seeking eye contact and chit chat with strangers.

Recently, feeling particularly invigorated and perhaps a bit randy after a yoga class – be careful girls, it happens– I ventured into the grocery store, still in my yoga attire, to grab just a few things. Making eye contact, saying hi, smiling, and then … I got a double take – hey now! Mama's still got it! Then the second double take. NICE! I finish up, get to the car, check the rear-view mirror – I don't really know why, to congratulate myself maybe? Who knows, but doing so is the only thing that kept me from making my next stop and pumping gas – with the purple pattern from my yoga mat transferred to my forehead. Nice.

There was a time when something as simple as that might have all but crippled me with embarrassment. Instead, this time I laughed.

And that, Mermaid, was indeed a good feeling.

But wait, there's more! Fast forward to another time, not feeling un-randy per se, but leaning more in that direction, and in my usual work

RULE #7
learn to laugh at yourself

attire of dusty paint-covered fabulousness and work boots, I run into Walmart to grab spaghetti squash. Now I LOVE LOVE LOVE spaghetti squash, so I always cook several at a time. I pick two, and not having thought to grab a cart, hug them against myself so I can have a free hand to grab one more thing and scoot over to the freezer cases.

I caught a glance or two from a couple of fellows and was slightly confused but really flattered(?). I turned into the next aisle and almost ran into one of them. Now this guy really checked me and took a gander straight at my chest (the same chest that I now know requires the smallest paddle available to properly perform a mammogram). I apologize for almost mowing him down, he gives me a full on twinkle of the eye with a half-smile and nods – a look I don't recall ever having seen at all, let alone seen shot in my direction since the late '90s. I halfway expected him to say, "How YOU doin'?"

Now you'd think after the yoga mat incident my radar would have gone off sooner, but it took all that time for me to look down and realize just exactly what two spaghetti squash with the stems pointing directly forward appear to be when hugged against one's chest. It was as close as I will ever be to a double D, and it was fun while it lasted.

See you when you get here.

your turn ...

learn
to laugh
at
yourself

What was your most embarrassing moment? Why?
When you do laugh at what is happening are you able to
keep it fun, or does it become self-deprecating?
Are you able to recognize your quirks as being some of
the most special parts of YOU?

7

learn to laugh at yourself

7

learn to laugh at yourself

7

learn to laugh at yourself

date _____

Amy Hege Atwell

RULE #8
redefine badass

Then, in November, I got hurt. Loading up after a show. Miserable, uncomfortable, "scary because I'm not really sure what's happening" hurt. After spending the night in that condition, and having promised myself that if whatever it was didn't pass by the morning, I would go to the ER. First thing, and in that much more pain, we did.

In the grand scheme of things, I was told that what had happened was not that big of a deal. A quick procedure would alleviate the pain and I could head home and return to work the next day, a little sore but none the worse for wear. I didn't go in bleeding, but after what I was told was an accidental "snip of an artery," and a struggle to stop the bleeding, I was discharged and sent on my way. We didn't get far before we were back, soaked from the waist down in my own blood, shivering uncontrollably, scared, yet strangely calm.

When the ER nurses got me undressed, one gasped. It took them awhile to stop the bleeding this time, and then even longer to finish the paperwork. I was discharged again, this time with a prescription for pain meds ("Here, I can tell by looking at you you're starting to hurt, so I'm going to give you a little gift") and the instructions that, because I'd lost a lot of blood, I "might want to eat a steak or some

RULE #8
redefine badass

beans for dinner."

I spent the better part of the next eight weeks in bed. Those eight weeks completely changed my life and I spent A LOT of time thinking through what was most important to me going forward. I made some life altering decisions during those two months. It still makes me tear up to think about it and I don't think I could say it any better if I tried … so I'm reprinting two blogs I made during that time.

Post from the Painted Mermaid, December 4, 2019

I spent so many of my young years being nervous – no, correction, afraid. Afraid to mess something up, afraid to make someone angry, afraid to look "stupid" doing something new. And then I became a Mommy. And that made me so much braver. It was HUGE to do SO many of the same things with someone so tiny to protect, and I began to "just do" – no choice, just DO. And then I began to gather a circle of friends who, without even trying, offered a whole new level of support. One in particular gave a whole new insight into myself and what I COULD do whereas in the past, without even realizing it, so much had been on what I COULDN'T.

Now don't get me wrong, even in hindsight I feel I've always been a positive person, but sometimes things around you – jobs, circumstances, even people – negatively influence you in ways you don't quite see. But these new influences were life changing in a good way. Not only did I grow brave, but I fancied myself as "tough." So I had a setback a couple of weeks ago. A large loss of blood put me in a place of reduced stamina and moments of dizziness from the anemia – things I've been lucky enough to have never been dealt. But I'm healing and recovering and being grateful for SUCH wonderful people around me. And nervous. Nervous to do so many of the things that were once so simple.

RULE #8
redefine badass

Nervous realizing even a "badass" can get hurt.

So what's my point Sunshine?

My point is this. It happens, and it's OK to be nervous. In fact, it's OK to be downright afraid.When that happens, just breathe, phone a friend, take whatever little step you can to push through at your own pace, but keep going – you'll get there.

And when you are strong, BE that friend.

Reach out and send a laugh or give a hug because you know what?

It really doesn't take much to make a difference for someone else. So today is a big day. I got clearance from Doc One yesterday, and if Doc Two seconds it this morning, I'm off to yoga – with a chair for support – this afternoon. If he doesn't, we try again next Wednesday.

Either way, as one of my fabulous friends said to me the other day, it's time to "redefine badass."

And just know that when you're ready, you can too.

Om Shanti Sunshine … See you when you get here.

Post from the Painted Mermaid, January 6, 2020

"Change is hard at first, messy in the middle and gorgeous in the end."

– Robin Sharma.

Oh my goodness Sunshine, how could you not be excited about a whole new DECADE?? Not even just a whole new year, but a whole new TEN!! And I don't know about you, but things changed for me this last year A LOT – in almost a "hurry up, we've got a lot to wrap up before we hit the new decade" kind of way.

Even though a good bit of it was like being gob smacked and gut punched, as the dust settles and the pieces all fall into place, I go "ohhhh, copy that.

I get it now". So once again I realize change IS good. Not always in the beginning. In fact, it can be SO hard in the beginning it feels like the world is going to end. Hard to wrap your head around, hard to digest, hard to

RULE #8
redefine badass

even breath.
And it most certainly can get messy in the middle
– painful, awkward, hollow, even empty.
But it's what you DO with that middle that makes the rest
GORGEOUS.
It's how you work that evolution; it's how you CHOOSE to GROW.
It's how you SEIZE the moment.

So be strong in your convictions Sunshine. Sow great seeds in the empty holes. Make the conscious effort to be OK with being alone, or the third wheel, or wholly and completely changed forever. When whatever it is, is no longer new, and whatever you've done with it is no longer right – be OK with change. Take what you want, leave the rest, and MAKE THE CHANGE. Maintain peace in knowing that if you let it, one way or another, it will ALWAYS be gorgeous in the end.

Good Morning, Sunshine … See you when you get here.

your turn ...

redefine badass

EVERYBODY has at least one "badass superpower." What is yours? (If you can't answer that, ask someone close to you, believe them, then OWN it!)

Are you concerned that you have lost yours? Or that it's changing?

How can you regain your superpower, or change it to fit your new needs/world?

Is there anything you need to let go of to make this happen?

redefine badass

date _____

redefine badass

date _____

_____

_____

_____

_____

_____

_____

_____

_____

_____

_____

_____

_____

_____

_____

_____

_____

_____

_____

date _____

Amy Hege Atwell

RULE #9
embrace your true beauty

If someone asked what I found physically attractive in others, my immediate response would always be the eyes and the smile. While I am a SUCKER for great eye contact from either gender, the two are hard for me to separate. Still, the eyes are indeed the window to the soul and a twinkle in the eye will melt me to the core in no time. When I look back at all the men to whom I've been attracted (that sounds like a lot doesn't it?? But hey I didn't marry the second time until I was 27 and even then I was married, not dead). There were plenty that did not possess – in fact I'd say probably none – your traditional Adonis-like traits, or at least not across the board. But they ALL had great eyes, a great smile, and a fantastic sense of humor. To my husband's great credit, this is something we could often discuss comfortably … because he wasn't dead either. I could see his reaction to "beautiful women," and I'm sure he could see my reaction to my "beautiful men." It was indeed one of the many things we did do well together – nothing inappropriate on any level, just a unique ability on both our parts to allow each other not only be human, but to acknowledge the need to feel attractive to the opposite sex … a need which lasts, I suspect, until the day you die.

So here's my question, Mermaid. If we as women accept and are

RULE #9
embrace your true beauty

frequently downright DRAWN to big men with teddy bear bellies and bald heads, certain odd features or downright terrible taste in clothes, why is it that we don't allow ourselves the same "shortcomings"?

How indeed can so many of those men say the most wonderfully outrageous things (I am SUCH a sucker for a harmless flirt – just ask Mark, that's one of the many reasons I married him in the first place) and not be the least apologetic for the fact that they are covered with paint, or haven't shaved for days?

I don't know either, Mermaid. The difference in how women are portrayed in the media? How our mothers felt about themselves and passed on to us? How things did or didn't go the first time we let a male person see us naked? You tell me, but one thing's for sure: we OWE it to ourselves and our partners to be confident with WHO we are, and confident in WHY they have chosen to be with us.

If for whatever reason you are uncomfortable with how you look or feel, do whatever it takes to make the changes that makes sense for you, NOT the boyfriend from 20 some-odd years ago who said "you'd be a real knock out if you'd lose a few pounds" as you modeled your new bathing suit. Let's commit to being genuinely US, ALL the time, before, during and, heaven help us, after marriage. (This point was made that much clearer to me by the fellow who revealed he was in his third marriage and, after our conversation told me, "I think you're great – at least for now!" with a laugh.)

And gentlemen, I must say there are no doubt plenty of you out there to whom this also applies. We might joke about the guy in the magazine or on the billboard, but stop and think – if I tell you I think Donald Sutherland and Adam Sandler are indeed just as hot as Sam Elliott – doesn't that tell you something? (And yes, I'm referring to bad

RULE #9

embrace your true beauty

boy Dirty Dozen era and beyond DONALD Sutherland.)

I suspect even Sam has SOMETHING he feels uncomfortable about – OK, no. Probably not Sam, but you get my point. We should ALL get over ourselves in the mirror, on the beach and in the bedroom. We should concentrate on the CONNECTION and recognize that beauty and attraction has more to do with how we respond to each other and how we make each other feel as human beings than it does with whether you have on mascara.

It's WHO YOU ARE and how you carry yourself that draws others to us, in as much as how you're built or what you wear. A truly fabulous and completely eye-opening conversation with a male friend summed it up perfectly when he vehemently insisted, "We hate it when you ask if we think you're attractive. Of course we think you're attractive! The least attractive thing about you is that YOU don't think you're attractive!"

After that same conversation, I came to realize and put into words how I truly never recognized the depth of my own beauty until I saw it in my own child. This is really hard to explain, but I look at him and don't see a single flaw. If I happen to notice the slight scar from a fall when he was two, it reminds me of the time I was terrified of what awful thing had happened to this little person I love so dearly. When I see his now faded birthmark I think of all the wonderful comments from strangers when he was tiny about how their baby had had one similar, and what they called it and how theirs too had faded – and the look in their eyes as they smiled and walked down their own memory lanes.

I find my cowlicks maddening, but his endearing – and they are all but the same. I love his sense of humor and the RIDICULOUS faces

107

RULE #9
embrace your true beauty

he makes. I love that he whistles and I know just exactly what kind of wrinkles that will leave – and that he makes up his own songs just like his Daddy did when we were first dating.

I love that he loves music and art. And I know when – for whatever reason the mood strikes him – he comes up to me and puts his little boy hand on my 50-(almost 51, Punkin')-year-old stomach that no amount of yoga will ever make taut again and says in a silly voice with a funny face "I like your squishy belly" before running off. I know that he MEANS it, and I love that.

I see how people react to him and I know where he got some of those faces and that sense of humor. I recognize the depth of his beauty … and therefore my own.

It's a shame that at some point, we somehow lose the confidence that our mates APPRECIATE all of our physical imperfections because they are parts of what they love more – our sense of humor, our ability to sing or play an instrument, our ability to see potential in a discarded item and turn it into something new, the way we can cook a fabulous meal, or roller skate. Even more so, the way we make them feel when we genuinely laugh at their jokes, or legitimately show interest in whatever it is they love, paying attention and making real eye contact when they speak.

And I kid you not, during this same discussion with my male friend the Pina Colada song comes up! (If you don't know it, now is your chance to learn something new, Mermaid! Google away!) As the song goes, a married man has gotten so bored in his relationship that he takes out a personal ad listing all the things he loves in a potential partner. And when the person who responds shows up, well guess who?

RULE #9
embrace your true beauty

Why do we let life get so in the way that we not only stop doing the things we love as individuals, but we stop doing the things we love together? When was the last time you thought about what you love to do, let alone asked your spouse?

What if the better question is not a question but a command? What if "Tell me what you love most about me" replaced the question "Do you think I'm fat?" Be ready for him to take a minute to figure it out because, let's be honest, at this point he MIGHT know not to say "your squishy belly," but he probably doesn't really understand why! (And ladies, one male friend told me he loves his wife's stomach – about which she complains – because the little change that's there reminds him she gave him two beautiful boys. She won't believe him ... but I could tell by the look on his face, he spoke the truth.)

Or try a different question entirely, like "Hey, after the kids go to Grandma's, are we going at it up against the wall in the hallway or on the kitchen table?"

You and he both know the odds are pretty high it's neither – but maybe it eases you in to the topic and makes one or both of you laugh, and if you're lucky, your question gets an equally ridiculous retort.

Finally, what if "Dammit I hate it when you (fill in the blank)" becomes a genuine "I love how you (fill in the blank with the opposite)." And what if we finally just TALK with EACH OTHER about the big white elephant in the room – KNOWING the white elephant is just an expression, and NOT US either literally nor figuratively??? I think it all boils down to this – it is frequently the lack of confidence in ourselves that is indeed the root of many, many things that aren't on track. Figuring that out for ourselves can indeed be tough. Just because you find said confidence doesn't mean that at

RULE #9
embrace your true beauty

some point it won't again be shaken. It is the person who ACTS on that awareness that moves the needle, Mermaid, and it truly does not matter how hard or fast you move that needle, but simply that you do.

See you when you get here.

your turn ...

embrace
your true
beauty

What are your best qualities? Why?

What is your favorite physical feature? Why?

What do you do every day to look/feel your best? (yoga or other workout? meditation? healthy food? time with a good book or hobby?)

Are you honoring your own beauty or neglecting it?

9

embrace your true beauty

date _____

embrace your true beauty

9

embrace your true beauty

date _____

embrace your true beauty

Amy Hege Atwell

RULE #10
be OK with being human

Putting all of this down on paper has done amazing things for me. Pushing back from the table and digesting the events after the fact gives clarity for me to see them in a slightly different light. I have allowed myself to be proud of what I handled well, learn from what could have gone differently, and know that both were what I was capable of giving and doing at the time. This, I think, is true for all of us.

Just how pulled together we feel depends on the day, or just how well equipped we are able to handle even the daily tasks at hand. Sometimes I wonder, by the sheer nature of putting out there a blog post or wow, a BOOK, that I am somehow implying that I have it all together all the time ... and that is simply not the case.

I believe the term for that these days is "Imposter Syndrome." Although I have my brief moments of worry, I'm not an imposter Mermaid, and neither are you. If you're putting on a brave face because you're going through something or you're choosing to only look at the positive instead of wallowing in the negative, that's not being an imposter, that's being you. For the record that's the kind of human I WANT to be. I WANT to keep my brave face on when things are hard because, quite frankly, it makes those hard times easier for

117

RULE #10
be OK with being human

ME.

These days I realize that when things are hard, revealing that to others is OK, perhaps even critical; doing so not only lets you be OK with the fact that you are human, but lets others see that you are OK with the fact that you – AND they – are ALL in fact HUMAN. Just don't get stuck there. Switch from the venting of problems to finding solutions or taking action as soon as possible, knowing that things may come in waves. Especially when the hard things we face are often so VERY hard.

So take off the superhero cape a minute, Mermaid, and stop and think. Did someone ASK you to put on that cape? Or did you pick it off the rack all by yourself? Regardless, take that damned thing off, visualize yourself burning it and blowing away the ashes.

Be OK with being human and I'll see you when you get here.

your turn ...

be OK with being human

What upset you this week?

Who 'took advantage of you'?

Did you agree to something you wish you hadn't?

Who asked to do it? Why did you say yes?

What could you / should you do differently next time?

10

be OK with being human

be OK with being human

10

be OK with being human

date _____

be OK with being human

I have learned SO MUCH over the past two and a half years. Lessons that will without a doubt serve me well for what I hope will be many years to come. I know in my heart that every event happened – and continues to happen – just exactly how and when it is intended and that following and trusting in the steps as they've been revealed has brought me to a much better place. I dare say a much better place for all. So embrace the hard times and don't force or rush yourself through them; they are a huge part of what makes you who you are. By the same token, don't wallow in them ... for they aren't what defines you.

Take your knocks, eat your spinach first (an expression that came from my mother teaching me to do what's right and consume the least favorite thing on my plate first before it gets cold and completely hard to swallow) and move through it. Then kiss whatever it is goodbye and move on.

Forgive yourself your "sins," be they real or imagined, give them back to the universe and just move on. Punishing yourself – or them – forever serves no purpose. Opening yourself to the possibilities of tomorrow not only serves a purpose, but indeed the greater good.

So rest easy Mermaid, and I'll see you when you get here.

epilogue

The day came when my gut told me to send a copy of the book in its current state to Carol. I rarely argue with my gut these days and despite my usual style of working whatever it is until my eyes bleed in hopes of receiving ridiculous amounts of praise due to its level of perfection, I did send the manuscript to Carol.

When Carol and I talked, she pointed out that I had forgotten #9 and that the "only thing it might be missing" might be something about finding your home and how to find your home. We batted around a couple of thoughts, and I remembered each time we had discussed the working title, she always spoke about loving the water, particularly the ocean and literally crying at times when she would leave vacations to return inland.

The timing was interesting indeed because at the same time I hit send on the email, I was also desperately trying to find a new place to move with my little one. The 6-month lease we had taken as a family of three (plus mother-in-law) was in anticipation of the new home we were building together being completed. The lease was ending and we had only just broken ground on the house.

We were going into the high season in a tourist town, and although the owners of the home in which my son and I were staying had said we could continue on month-to-month, the rent was far too much for me to handle solo. I also had concerns they may want or need the home for their own enjoyment before our house was complete.

There was seemingly nowhere to be found – I had checked everywhere including campgrounds. Running in the background was news of a virus causing deaths and some closings. After hitting send, I literally found and took a new rental, moved and unpacked us. Schools were closed, traffic dropped dramatically at The Painted Mermaid, the word Pandemic was being used and I was forced to have my Mermaids apply for unemployment.

Unknowingly, I had reached out and made an online friend who at some point revealed her super power for which I was all of the sudden in desperate need. She had the ability to simplify online website/store set-ups for the modern day impaired, and I hadn't officially tried to sell anything from my dormant website in years. I found myself stumbling through a RIDICULOUS process to get internet at the new address so we could home-school (all the while falling further and further behind there) and partnering with as many artists as I could to determine next steps. During this time I was completely and utterly amazed, despite all the chaos, at just how much this new place felt like home. And when I woke up suddenly at just about midnight the day before going under a 30-day stay at home directive, I went to the computer. I found that I hadn't forgotten Rule #9, it was there all along. I must have sent her a previous copy? And had I not done so, who knows where my thoughts may have gone over those seven days, but here's where they landed.

Home is indeed where the heart is, Mermaid. It is the place that gives you peace no matter how big or small, cluttered or tidy. Home is more about a feeling than the shelter. It is about the energy it absorbs and the energy it imparts. If you feel yourself being inexplicably drawn to an area or a place, know that there is a reason. Memories from a past life? Guidance from God? The pull of the Universe? Or simply the pleasure invoked from a scene in a movie? Who's to say?

And who's to argue? Just know that your gut is there for a reason, as is your heart, and to those you should always listen – about everything really, but ESPECIALLY about home.

Because Mermaid, there is absolutely, unequivocally, without a doubt, no place like home.

See you when you get here.

ADDITIONAL RESOURCES

The Paleo Way - Documentary Series with Pete Evans

It's Not Your Money by Tosha Silver

Sara Conner Tanguay, Wartooth Designs

Miriam Lane, Balanced Bodies

Emily Silverman Yoga, Leland, NC

Mert Wray, Pink Moon Yoga, Oak Island, NC

Shannon Dievendorf, Rebel Soul Yoga, Oak Island, NC

Shannon Gordon, Bikes and Bags, Southport, NC

Candice Murphy, Cape Fear Fitness, Southport, NC

Jonathan Branch, Must Have Rust, High Point, NC

10 LITTLE RULES

Stay connected to
the 10 Little Rules Community

Like and Follow our Facebook
page at facebook.com/10LittleRules
for ongoing support and discussion on
how to apply these books to living your best life

Visit our website for updates
at www.10littlerules.com

<u>Books in the 10 Little Rules series:</u>
10 Little Rules for a Blissy Life by Carol Pearson
10 Little Rules for Your Creative Soul by Rita Long
10 Little Rules of Hank by Wendy Price
10 Little Rules for Finding Your Truth by Micki Beach
10 Little Rules for Mermaids by Amy Hege Atwell
10 Little Rules for the Modern Southern Belle by Beverly Ingle

Watch for more 10 Little Rules books launching soon!

Made in the USA
Columbia, SC
18 July 2020